It Is Abnormal
TO BAN POETRY

It Is Abnormal
TO BAN POETRY

Dara Kalima

Copyright © 2025 by Dara K. Marsh.
All rights reserved. This book or any portion thereof may not be reproduced or used in any manner whatsoever without the express written permission of the publisher except for the use of brief quotations in a book review.
Printed in the United States of America

Cover by Dara K. Marsh

First Printing, 2025

ISBN: 978-0-9985020-4-5

For permission requests contact the publisher at: darakalima@gmail.com

DEDICATION

For those that lit the torch, carried it, passed it on...

*...and for those now picking it up,
there's still a ways to go.*

TABLE OF CONTENTS

Never Forget	1
History's Obsession	6
The Wordy Construction of a Duplex	7
Where To Put You?	8
Per Didi to Gogo	9
The Erudite's Mastery of Words	11
Unsettling Birth	13
How Am I?	15
Precious Moments	18
Threads And Threats	19
An Abridged Account of My Encounters with Racism	21
Pressure V Pipes	24
Taj In Manhattan	26
Coffee And Bagel	27
The Price of Negroland	28
Approaching Anubis' Scale	30
The Taste	31
Cautionary Tale: William Lewis Moore	32
Pounding	34
Today's Poem	36
Make Believe	37
Bodies Found in Ukraine? Taiwan? USA?	39
Pavement Sandwich	41
Reconciling Thoughts	43
Black	45
An Interrobang with A Semicolon Ending	49
In The Zendo 3-12-24	52
1970s Dangerous	54
Elevated Playbook	57
For Emmett, Dick, Haywood, And All Accused	59
Same Shit Different Pigeon	60
Why Come?	63
Nothing Is	65
My Award Winner	66

The Graveyard	69
And If This Whole Experience Wasn't a Metaphor…	71
Respite	74
The Night That Didn't Happen	78
This Very Moment	80
Dreamscape	83
No Soliciting	85

NEVER FORGET

They say never forget,
like we in NY can ever forget,
like we haven't tried.
We can't.
Our skyline has a keloid.
Photographs depict before and after,
of when two eventually became one.

They say never forget 9/11 like they say
never forget the Alamo or the Holocaust.
At what cost are we to remember?

Are we not triggering decades' old PTSD?
Were you here?
Were you there?
Do you remember the fear,
the night terrors,
and the domestic terrorists that
terrorized my Muslim friends, again,
like they did post car bomb?

Do you remember these moments?
Where were you when mosques became targets?
When white men were made gods,
forgetting the others slain.
Blacks were also lost,
and East Asians, and Latines,
South Asians, Middle Easterners,
males, females,
trans persons and nonbinary folks!
And there's the atheists, the Christians,
the Jews, Sikhs, Buddhists, Wiccans,
the Hindus, and the Muslims too!
Do you say the names of all?

Do you pray for each?
Or just the firemen?
And policemen?
Do you still light a candle
for the young Mexican
that still dreams of piles of shoes,
heaps of skin, and blinding ash,
the man, that was barely an adult,
who put his lungs on the line to try and save
just one...
Do you list him among your heroes?

Do you think of the colleague
that gave their life to stay with their friend
that was disabled?
And do you name the inventors
that spread cloth wings
with hopes of soaring...
Did you think of those frozen in flight?

Or stuck in transit?
Remember those that walked home,
or the ones that didn't know
how to get back into their city
because they worked just outside it?
Ever listen to the remembrances
of those that traveled by ferry?

Do you think of the family that got the last calls,
or missed that final ring,
those whose voicemails were too full for the message?
Or the ones in the crowds that ran...

Do you give a damn about those
who would forget if they could,
that pray they can?

How dare you demand they remember?

They remember.

They remember the taste
of their breaths though baited
as they hoped their loved one was
on a lower floor, that they weren't trapped,
that they didn't take that particular train, and
emerged from the other exit,
as they waited for a message saying,
"I'm home..."
They remember...

Just like they remember the victims of today,
or yesterday, and the countless from yester years.
My dear, they remember... But do you?

When flashing only images of those in red or blue?
Do you say any of the other names?
Do you say any other names?
Do you say their names?
Do you pray for those that feel guilty for surviving,
for calling out that day,
for being on vacation,
for not being assigned to that shift,
which made someone else be present?
These folks can't live in the present
because they can't forget...

Stop telling them to remember.

Stop telling me to remember.
I tried to forget it the moment it happened.
Tried to forget my boss screaming
in the empty store, and

the churning of my belly
as I assured Grandma that her grandson
probably wasn't at work just yet...
As I, too, awaited confirmation...
I can't forget how deafeningly silent or
reflective or woeful the bus was or how I
numbed myself with innocent movies
just to placate the fear-filled inner-child or
just to escape the constant replaying
of images I didn't want to see.

Nor can I escape memories of the smell
that wafted uptown in the aftermath
as we tried to escape into a theater for comfort...

I can't forget...

I can't forget September 11th,
just like I can't forget those lungs
that COVID ravaged, or
those Black lives that didn't seem to matter,
just like I can't forget that Indigenous lives matter
as much as Jewish lives do,
and are as precious as Palestinian lives.
Just like I can't forget
that Muslim lives are gifts.
And we shouldn't forget
that we are all American.

We can't forget America's history...
the parts that birthed this very enemy...
I can't forget the myriads of ways
we, here in this country,
birthed our victimhood,
whether it was because of Charlie Wilson's War,

Eugenicist's policies, or chattel slavery and manifested destinies...
This place always tampered in societies,
creating mass casualties both foreign and domestic...
Do you remember that?
Do you remember them?

If you require this day stay in memories,
you better remember those others.
And all those names.

Will you remember?
I sure as hell can't forget.

HISTORY'S OBSESSION

Your want
to call
the abnormality of the past
a normal worth returning to,
is proof
of your abnormal insanity,
and I,

I want **NO** part
of that "normalcy".

THE WORDY CONSTRUCTION OF A DUPLEX

I sat at the laptop pounding the keys
Words hemorrhage out painfully

    Hemorrhaging and spraying painfully
    Shedded linings demand retribution

Shredded lines and pages seek retribution
Words once friendly now cold and distant

    Words, once comforting turned frigidly distant
    I miss when we, together, danced effortlessly

Longing for when we danced effortlessly
In this moment, I feel like Atlas holding worlds

    Now, as Atlas, I struggle to hold the world
    One wrong word, everything shatters and scatters

No wrong words, else all shatters and scatters
I sit, at the laptop, pounding still at the keys.

WHERE TO PUT YOU?

On the shelf?

                                                                                    ON PROBATION?

                In fantasy?

                                                      In a poem?

        S c a t t e r e d across pages?   On timeout?

                                            …On s p e e d d i a l?

                As part of my prayers?

My penance?

                                          `In the inner circle?`

        On the other side of the line?
              Third in line?
FIRST?

                                                              Dead last.

On the do not contact list?

                              In my heart?

Out my mind?

                                         <u>Underfoot?</u>

                    Or in between my legs?…

PER DIDI TO GOGO

You inquire,
why we are here?
Why *we* are here?
Why are we here?
I can't say.

I hadn't asked to be,
but you know how it goes...
lovers blend bodies unprotectedly,
unexpectedly producing progenies,
or maybe I am here because God decided
she needed a crafty community-oriented poet
to whisper sense into souls otherwise too ignorant,
or I'm here because capitalism and sexism and
patriarchy made abortions so déclassé...
There's also the obvious and often omitted
ships stole humans and massas stole vaginas,
birthing babies whose names can be found
on the records, all being my ancestors,
making this hell home and
I am stuck just passing time.

Or I'm here and we are here not to wait for Godot but
to poetically bear witness to the collective insanity
that is graying our strands and shortening our life spans...

Today, a more adult adult, wailed in my ear
at news I divulged, and I bore witness
as a thunderous reality unrelentingly
hurricaned upon this helpless human.

Now you, yes you,
have become witness to a shared disbelief
that morphed into visceral grief.

And maybe that's why we are here.
Because all of this is arduous,
but it's a modicum easier
when not traveling alone.

THE ERUDITE'S MASTERY OF WORDS

I want to write a poem written with,
no, dripping with three syllable words
and such great imagery
just to prove that I can master both,
that I'm more verbose
than my typical verse suggests.
I want my words to evoke pictographs that
tickle and stimulate your cerebrum,
persuading you to align your thinking with mine
even if only for a moment as my balladry
inspires one's synapses to spark critical thought
but I fear that the ramifications of descending too deeply
into hyperbole will steer us towards analogy filled
dead ends, missing opportunities for proper
understanding of my phraseology or parlance
into my particular truths. I mean, after all,
the two shortest sentences in the English language
are often misinterpreted. The first is the shortest of them,
no. No is a complete sentence whose definition
is often skewed, warped, and contorted into
the next shortest sentence, yes. Opposing definitions
often mixed to the benefit of the hopeful or more so
determined beneficiary.

Case in point,
I said no.
I said,
"no."
Using the word to be the negative answer to a request;
to simply state the requestor was not to get their way.
I said no
just like many before and after but
it mutated and translated itself into "yes"
in the ears of the receiver.

I said no again
and again
and again.
I even followed that with the action of using full force
to try to make space between us two but *no* somehow
repeatedly morphed into *yes* as it entered into his ear canal.
And since all he could hear was *yes*,
after a sequence of *nos*,
after much duress,
I finally said the same...

So, if the shortest sentence could be so misunderstood
why obfuscate my message in mixed metaphors
leaving things to the recipient's interpretation,
especially when the shortest sentence
that should not be easy to blur,
still seems quite obscure.

I'd love to write a poem with big words
but there's just too much at stake
to leave the understanding
in the hands of fate.

UNSETTLING BIRTH

There is a poem in my chest
trying to claw its way out,
like the baby alien,
though maybe
it's not in my chest,
maybe it's in my throat,
trying to give voice to my speechlessness,
and if it's not there,
maybe it's trapped
beneath my cranium.
That would explain the pain in my head
that's been throbbing.
Could it be contractions?
Labor pains.
This thought process is laborious.
Synapses stretching to connect the messages...
    what is the message?

Is it a lament dedicated to those that have trapped me in an annual two-month-cycle of grief. Should I write of how every winter, every other week they torment my cells with relentless sadness? It's been decades now... Or was it only moments ago? My body aches like it was seconds ago. Is this poem for my late cousin? Grandfather? Sister? For the embryo I named Stomach Flu?

                        or

              is it for the boy?
        For the tall handsome boy,
for the tall and handsomely nostalgic boy
              the boy that
           at every moment
       resembles a tossed coin?
     He's always bringing me hope

and suspense.
One side means winning his attention,
the other means...

AN ELLIPSIS!

...this poem feels like an ellipsis. a thought, half complete, a half-born baby seeing what is to come, trying to return from whence it came and my brain is working overtime to push out what feels to be crawling inside but it just won't flow out, won't be birthed. this poem. this poem. this slippery poem. just might kill me. if i apply too much more pressure pushing...

to push, we stop breathing. i don't feel like i am breathing, but i'm making no progress and my head keeps throbbing. there is a poem in here. i can feel it squirming.

Or

Maybe my insides are just still settling after realizing, and admitting to self and an audience, that even as a child, not even a decade in, I never found myself dreaming in love songs or rehearsing my own romcom. Never seeing tenderness formatively taught me early I was not worthy. My heart was only to pump salty tears. Exploding cars extinguished with superhero breath felt more tangible than romantic love. And so far, it's been not just belief...................it's been..truth.

Putting words, vulnerable sad words
from the subconscious and never spoken,
onto cold pages was like seeing my intestines
spread out full circle
still attached to my stomach and my rectum.
What a startling view it was.
So, maybe there was no poem,
maybe it was me, settling into the unsettling.

HOW AM I?

At the words, "how are you?"
I freeze with terror.
Answers rush towards my mouth
bottlenecking in my throat.
Eyes try to communicate on my behalf
but pressure forces expressions to well
blurring my vision with tears.
That question be the roll of dice
in a life-or-death game,
my heart rate goes tachycardic
as my mind attempts to process
the emotions and assesses
if it's safe to answer...
Can the asker hear that I'm crumbling?
Life is perpetual aftershocks.
Everything is falling off the walls.
I'm being buried under my clutter.
My room hasn't been clean in years.
I didn't want to get out of bed today.
Or yesterday.
I plan to stay in there tomorrow...

Work feels like a hamster wheel
and my joints are arthritic.
Do they care
that my body is betraying me?
Every month I lose more blood
than I can make...

My heart is being punished.
I am in love with a man
that is making me choose me over us
...each night...
I dream of returning to his arms.
I am an addict. My addictions...
boys, love, clutter, food, pain, busyness.
I'm so tired of being busy.
I am mad at myself
for waking up in time to turn off the gas
that my mom accidently left on...
I am pissed off at my parents
for being ordinary non-superhumans.
I'm angrier still at them for aging
and at my sister for dying.
This was her job...
It's more of a sentence than a gig.

I don't want any of this
and I shouldn't say a word
because I know I will be asked
for the umpteenth time
am I thinking of self-harm,
and while I'm not thinking of it now,
I fear the power of suggestion.
They'll think me crazy if I suggest
part of this is just the price of my melanin.
My bank account is empty.
And despite all of this
I'm generally okay.
I think... I mean...

I'm finally healing from the whiplash,
the scars from the tongue lashings
are mending.
No one died today
though I'm holding space
for friends losing people...
I'm carrying all of this
in atrophied arms and
on knees that creak so loudly
they wake me up at night,
I already get less than
5 hours of sleep on average.
There are just too many words or
maybe not enough...
Not sure if the asker is ready to listen.
I almost wish they'd not inquire
for I become a deer in a spotlight.
Please, flick the lights off
so I can go
run
hide.

PRECIOUS MOMENTS

She said,
      "People have issues."

I heard,
      "Enjoy your shoes."

We laughed,
      bellies jiggling,
      toes stomping,
      eyes pouring,

before realizing
I may be one
of those people
with issues
enjoying their shoes.

THREADS AND THREATS

It's quite peculiar
how frequently
my mental health
finds itself in
flux.
The angelic and demonic
and narcoleptic
w h h h h i s s s s p e r
and **YELL**
their bids
on my worth.
I traverse life
tightrope walking on
cooked spaghetti strings,
hoping their windy breath
doesn't tip *me* over.
My sanity is light
as a feather
though the thoughts be
weighty.
My progress
is a train derailing.
Sparked embers sometimes
grow and rage
furiously.
Can it be extinguished?
Dousing has only ever
paused it.
The concerns must be
saturated in positivity, but
I'm certain still
something will un-
do me.
The voices are trying.

I feel to be
unrave l i   n...
My mind
a skein of yarn and
those feuding
pull slowly while
untwisting the threads.
Is there even
a modicum of normalcy
out there for me? Or
will my wants forever be
eclipsed by
their reign over my body.
Who are they?
Who are they
to have a say?
How do I make them say less
so I can say more?

AN ABRIDGED ACCOUNT OF MY ENCOUNTERS WITH RACISM

1. In 5th or 6th grade the pastor at my school showed up in black face
2. Racism was written into my history books that talked more about Myles Standish than Samoset
3. And within the lessons that focused on John Brown and not Nat Turner
4. It showed up when our white Math/Gym teacher thought it appropriate to put his hands on a Black child in front of his classmates, like we would let him get away with that in a majority Black school
5. His mom used her privilege to yell at us kids for speaking up against his abusive behavior
6. Oh, in kindergarten my white presenting teacher punished me for wanting to learn more, how dare I?
7. I met racism in HS when I had to move to the mediocre math table that just happened to be browner because it was assumed I couldn't keep up with my friends
8. Racism hung out in the vacant brick lots I grew up seeing in the Bronx; rubble of property fires and community divestment
9. After a botched surgery, my surgeon didn't listen when I complained, nor did the lawyers. It took over two years of doctors visits and living in agony to get a diagnosis... they just refused to listen to this Black girl... yep, racism
10. I heard about it in Crown Heights
11. There was also that dude named Rodney King
12. The news that broke about Abner Louima broke my heart, made me outraged and taught me fear at the same time
13. I got passed up for a cab on my birthday, on my graduation day, on a regular day, probably yesterday and most definitely this coming weekend

14. Racism found me at my first job when I got paid less than a white man
15. It also found me when I walked into a different interview and they sighed when I arrived
16. And that other time when I sat in the waiting room for longer than the actual interview itself
17. Racism kicked me on the train without an apology
18. It also sat on my lap and squeezed me out of my seat
19. Sean Bell was a friend of a friend
20. Sandra Bland went to HS with a colleague
21. Racism ignored me when I tried to speak up
22. It asked me if I will ever get to just exist, as if I had any say in that and of course it meant to exist within white standards
23. Racism forgot to invite me on girls' trips locally and nationally
24. It stuck its fingers in my hair
25. At my job
26. At a fundraiser
27. At a retreat
28. Racism followed me around stores
29. It made my church a tourist stop
30. It made my poverty an ethnic attraction
31. It stood on my stairs and took photos
32. It told me my braids were acceptable but never get dreadlocks
33. Racism met me and my mom in a restaurant in Midtown Manhattan
34. And before I was born when mom was denied good grades because, you know, Black folks weren't allowed that
35. It also showed up at the fake abortion clinic in the Bronx that cared more about unborn Black fetuses than the actual circumstances of would be mothers or the resulting children born into suffering; thankfully I made it to the real clinic

36. And it was revealed to me when I realized why my great-grandmother could barely read.
37. Racism filled my lungs, limiting its ability
38. It tastes like quarter waters, potato chips, Sour Powers, canned veggies, fries, and pizza. It's the high fructose flavored, overly sugared and way too salty low-quality food that was cheap to eat because fresh food was literally too far out of reach and expensive to consume. Racism was terrible for my body, but yummy for my tongue.
39. And it exists in the huh's and dismissal of what I say, and the talking over of me and the demand that I switch my speech for their ears' ease
40. It found me the first day a stove-heated straightening comb touched my hair, and every time since that I had to "tame" my mane
41. Oh and racism met at...

Actually, this was only to be an abridged list because I could go on and on and on at length, and even as far back to when it met my great-great-great-great-great-grandmothers on ships and in tobacco fields because I still carry their DNA which means it met me then too

42. I have a date with it tomorrow as well...

PRESSURE v.
a contra-

My knees cry
each time, painful, in prayer
seeking answers & remedies.

My knees ache!
bending for the world
kneeling for the right to exist
marching for justice
lifting levers
at every possible chance.
Tirelessly,
isms
BANG, THUMP, THUD —
percussive dissonance
warring with my supple tissue,
internally.

Inhale soothing breath
exhale hurt
lift agonizing fog

to float away.

(medication)

"Help me
please
don't let me plummet..."

PIPES
-puntal

As I run to my therapist stressed
filled with hopeful desperation—
Help me!

This arthritic mind
always pressing down on me
while oppression reverberates
with statements about my worth
throughout my life. We hope
our lives will be priceless. But
toxicity & inequality
(sixty cents on every dollar earned)
clog dancing throughout my cranium,
an obstructive rhythm
my place, my rank, buried
within the canyons of my gray matter.

Ohm
repeatedly
Ohm
to decompress
to bring peace

Meditating: How much
will it take?
Can I just leave today on this couch?
I beg my therapist:
please
help me swim.

TAJ IN MANHATTAN

Every last Thursday,
we, in our dapper brownness,
trekked to the lively lounge,
ready to gulp and sway all away.

We eagerly seeking amnesia,
wanting to forget the bosses
and their demands, the children
and their demands, the racists
and their demands, the internalized critics
and their demands. We gulped
until the noise clicked off
and we sway away with the bass
setting our feet to hypnotic beats.

Who cares about yesterday or
the next day and their ultimatums
when we had this moment.
If nothing else, we had this,
each month, to forget and to live.

We would party until the hours turn old,
and until our inhibitions grow young.
Knees and responsibilities be damned!

This was our Thursday routine,
we got dapper with swagger and
swayed euphorically until dawn.

COFFEE AND BAGEL

So, you start your day with a steaming cup of espresso, extra strong and perfectly sweet just how you like it with your low-fat yogurt and your toasted everything bagel from that artisanal place just up the street with a nice helping of lox and scallion cream cheese ready for you to daintily bite with taste buds tingling from delight as if this feast wasn't a standard for you, like you didn't just have it yesterday and will not have more tomorrow. The delight really is in the ease of the morning as you look out of your floor to ceiling windows with a view of the river and the skyline on the other side. Your favorite song serenading you, courtesy of Alexa, who caters to your every whim and want... What a marvelous start to the day that has everything you could hope for in store. You take a small bite, chew 30 times as charm school taught you when you were a debutante, and the food flows slowly down your pristine esophagus which is something that Eric and George and
  70 others will
     never again experience
        because their throats were
          caught in a hold that made
            it non-functional, their existence
             non-viable to you, vital
               life signs undetectable
                 because of a legalized
                   murder probably done
                   because
                   you...

                called about the man with the cigarettes, or the water bottles, or the funny look, or the one that was bird watching, or doing their delivery job... but don't you fret about that.

                            You just enjoy that bagel.

THE PRICE OF NEGROLAND
inspired in part by Margo Jefferson's memoir

I've looked longingly at the remains of horizontal slits on transparent skin and then stared at where I imagine my veins rest beneath the melanin. Used to daydream of etching such paths towards eased pain but I only wanted to slice twice; wrist to inner elbow because a he broke my heart and I didn't think it would restart. Needed grief to be unshackled, needed the stale air in my lungs to be released and I wanted no more in return. Didn't want to return to a life without, but they say children, whose parents were committed to such a fate, commit to such paths too and what path then would my niece later choose, she being the closest I'd get to progeny.

I paved no ways, and I do not regret not doing it, but when I look at those beautiful, healed, crafty cuts on those translucent arms my brown irises morph to forest green. But there is no wish for the pain that led to the repeated act, of that, I have enough, for I understand the need for control, or the cry for help, or the attempt to feel something else, or the desire to finally take matters into your own hands, I understand the burden that makes you want to cut and run...

but I've never been allowed a vice.

No: alcohol, or weed, or cocaine, or sex, or anything.

Just: a lesson to always grit teeth and bare down but don't push, can't ever push, constrict your undercarriage, don't push it out and don't dare push back, just hold it in, smile, always smile, always smile with pearly whites beaming, and do not crack a tooth while tightly clenching teeth, hold it right there, just like that, don't even utter a sound, shed no tears either...

I imagine, from holding it all in for so long, that my insides look like a dreary hoarded abode: dust covered journals filled with lists of transgressions... the undigested and emaciated bones of self-worth and dreams jutting out of places with only traces of their skins. no meat... and there are piles and piles and piles and piles and piles and piles and piles and piles and piles of societal trash that's only partially composted over time... in corners, if there are such things, are smoldering electrical fires kept under control by their neighboring rivers of boiling bile... spiders and their webs fill any spaces or crevices left. There is no escape for the things... it all festers and ferments... until when, finally, my outsides join in on the rotting.

But...apparently......that is not yet.

And this is why I look on, enviously. Those scars mean, that even if done self-destructively, your hurts escaped and you found healing while we, while I, have never been afforded such a luxury.

APPROACHING ANUBIS' SCALE

Heart leadens,
from dragging carcasses
of the unsaved, unconvinced, unchanged.
Tethered to their fates.
Is heart lighter than feather,
when good deeds pave ways to hell?
Were they just and true?
Was I... pawn?...
Traversing this treacherous trail
towards the final scale,
cannot tell if tales were
fact, fiction, or contrived contradiction.
What was this life for?
Could I, should I have
accomplished more?
How much does a feather weigh?
From what was it plucked?
A beast bigger than my burden?
Life was hell,
can death be any worse?
Encumbrances increased?
Or does this process
shed distress?
Heart's heavy,
dragging stiff corpses
of regrets and undones.
Tell me, Anubis,
how heavy is this feather?

THE TASTE

Death tastes like quarter waters,
tainted water, potato chips,
canned foods, fries, and
dollar pizza. It's the high fructose
flavored, overly sugared,
polluted and way too salty
low-quality food that was cheap to get
because fresh food was literally too far
out of reach and expensive to eat.
It therefore tastes like high blood
pressure, diabetes and lead poisoning.
Or is that what murder tastes like?

Maybe then, death tastes like ash.
You know, that which we all return.
Frames reduce to powder, inevitably.
It may feel desert dry on the tongue,
our lips chapped, and in last moments
we beg for just a bit of moisture
like George pleaded for more air?

Or does it taste metallic?
Does your mouth fill with the taste
of iron as your life force slowly
exits the body. Your insides now
external after violence punctured you.

Could death instead, in fact, taste sweet
after having been released from
all this torturous human suffering.
I hope it's flavored like my favorite
caramel fudge ice cream consumed
on a sweltering labor-intensive day.
After all, life is just that when Black.

CAUTIONARY TALE: WILLIAM LEWIS MOORE

I.

White Male.
In Binghamton, NY, he first received mail.
Loved people, walking, and the mail.
He delivered mail.

And he stood in lines.
He saw no color lines.
He went to jail for those mixing lines.
He wrote truth on lines of lines for lines.
From Maryland to Alabama he drew lines.
Then walked along paved and mapped lines.

He shared synopses of his lines.
He crisscrossed and exed out colored lines.
For some he crossed the line.
Found himself in the bullet's fire line.
Blood ran down in fatal lines.

II.

White man seeing no color,
betrayed his color,
losing his color.
In seeing no difference between
Black and White,
he became blue.
All because he tried to deliver a message
in the form of a letter
about the fallacy of color inequality.
The color betrayer
betrayed the supreme supremacists.
Was killed like the niggers he loved.
Today, his "sins" would have been
displayed on trees
like those of those Rittenhouse slayed,
just like George Floyd,
like Michael Brown,
like Eric Garner,
like every nigger they've put down...
their existence criminal
for those folks were only three-fifths.
Blacks and their lovers can't be people.
Human card stripped.
Life defaulted.
This be the price of forsaking your race...

But
when Mooro was stopped,
29 more Moores continued his walk...
Attempting to deliver the message...
Millions still take steps to deliver this memorandum
MOORE will walk tomorrow...
Assault rifles won't stop Moore's March.

POUNDING

My feet lose their familiar footing.
They clumsily explore paths they should know intimately,
but they trip, stumbling and bumbling around.
Lost.
They are lost.
They lost something...
someone...
their dance partner?
Was there ever a partner?
Was there ever really a dance?
Could any feet do more than
cake walk with steps forced
for amusement of others, lest whips find dermis,
sculpting more branches on keloid trees.
Will the feet-less man on the horse catch up?
Will feet not make it across the watery way to
makeshift villages of hope
...hope lost, forgotten, mistaken...
the feet walked many miles to this place
ignoring the sprains sustained
from the prickly promise-covered pebbles.
They traversed much in hopes of sanctuary.
Sanctuary is a fallacy in places with short memories,
places that keep forgetting purchases
and wars won on Black backs...
the feet hoped naively that
memories would speak to greater angels,
but they took bad angles,
and as they stepped they lost footing.
Feet lost footing.
They didn't stop though.
They won't stop.

They march.

We march,
hopefully towards justice,
or at least some semblance of sanctuary.
Maybe the lost footing
will be recovered by feet?
Hopefully.

TODAY'S POEM

This poem,
yes,
this poem is
brought to you by
nothing.
Nothing...
Not one thing
which is what
I feel to have,
nothing
or maybe
it's ashes.
Yes,
that!
This poem
is brought to you
courtesy of ashes.
Ashes from each
ambition and hope
and goal
burned to nothing
but ash.
There were many,
but society... and racism... and sexism... and slights...
and doubt... and chipping... and shreds... and sickness...
and kindling... and death... and hate... and matches...
So,
yes,
ashes.
And what
can be built from that?

Not even poetry.

MAKE BELIEVE

There's scabs on my back
again.
To feel them, to
pick at them, I
slinky stretch my middle-aged arms.
There's several,
arrived in the wee hours.

I pretend
they are marks of passion.
He left them on me
in gratitude for what I'd done to him
or to not slip too far into
euphoria
while taken to places of safety.
There's no safety here.
We can't afford to forget this.
Scabs were
the price of pleasure,
of escapism.

i. pretend.

I pretend they are love marks,
not blotches of punishment.
Not the self-mutilation done
when unconsciously internalizing
the tongue whippings
self-proclaimed superiors gifted.
They are not kind enough
to rip apart my back manually so
they make talons of my night nails.
I sleep-claw at the pressure place.

Blue satin pajamas, scarlet.
More scabs arrive come morning.

i. pretend.

I say it's just flared eczema,
knowing it is misplaced stress,
while wishing they were
souvenirs of his loving.

BODIES FOUND IN UKRAINE? TAIWAN? USA?
(to the tune of Baa Baa Black Sheep)

Madam, Madam?
Have you seen my kin?
    Oh dear, oh dear,
    Check therein?
    One bag's a neighbor,
    One bag's unknown...
And one might be him, but there's
many in this zone.

                        Leader! Leader!
                        Why'd you start this war?
                                Power! Power!
                                What else for?
                        Success should be near
                            They are to fold
                    And when I win, the total
                          deaths won't be told.

Madam. Madam.
Have you seen my kin?
    Oh, dear. Oh dear,
    Check therein...

                      Commander! Commander!
                      Was it worth the price?

                          Of course! Of course!
                              We'd pay thrice!!
                  Resistance's grown large,
                        this we must quell!
                        They won't deny me,
                        We're too strong to fail.

Madam! Madam!
Have you seen my kin?
    Oh dear! Oh, Dear...
    Check therein.
    That bag's a teacher,
    That bag's just bones.
    That might be him, there's many
    bodies in this zone...

              Madam... Madam?
              Have you seen my kin?
                            Oh, dear... oh... dear...

PAVEMENT SANDWICH

There are carcasses,
everywhere,
where there should be gold
speckling the sleepless streets —
carcasses.

"Natives" were told
the foreign bodies are invaders,
are hungry hostiles,
are going to damage the ecosystem,
as if it weren't already bruised,
as if we couldn't find harmony,
as if their produce would be poison,
not fruit.

They told all,
Kill on sight.
Kill sans prejudice.
Kill.
Make carcasses of the immigrants.
To make streets safe,
Kill.
Speckle and spot streets with bodies.

Think not of the bodies,

the other bodies,
the ones paved upon.
Bones
under the parks,
that too
were tied to lives feared.
Lives that too
had no value to the majority.

Lives that too
were an invasion thwarted...
Can't have them taking over.
Can't change the natural way of things.

Both groups were delivered via cargo,
Both were casualties of commerce,
Both sandwich NYC pavement.

RECONCILING THOUGHTS
for Eternity

I'd like to think their exit
was like the 75 Igbos —
the legendary flying Africans.

With steadfast determination
that their existence
would not be defined
by faith-filled sadistic oppressors,
ceremoniously they
marched into Dunbar Creek
sprouting wings and or fins
guided towards destiny.

I wonder, was my friend's exit like that?
An act of rebellion against those
who tried to define their life,
using religion as an excuse?
Hope it was not a fight for peace
that made them flee these shores.

There's no way to know,
but I would like to think
they enjoyed some funny videos,
ate a hearty vegan meal,
wrote their final messages,
raised two fingers
at those that did them dirty
and strode away as if clean,
and then
as their final act
of Black magic
slipped out of their flesh
transforming into something

even more stunning
more breathtaking
more majestic and mythical
than they'd already been.

I'd like to think that.

BLACK

Black is
both
the
absence of and
an amalgam of
all the colors...
Like the space
where the gravity
is so strong nothing exists is called
black
but if you mix
all the paints
or
color over the same spot
with all the crayons
you get black.
Black is therefore
the absence and presence of all,
black must also be
the beginning
and ending of all.
Black is the comfort
of the night,
where your tears can hide.
Black is the coal
that ignites the fire.
Black creativity
is birthed
from the blackness
of others' ire.
Black is tired.
Black people
are tired.
Black people

are dying.
Black people
have yet to matter.
Black binds vision,
black holes lack
transparency and operate
in opacity.
Shadows and night limit
one's sight
forcing one
to rely on touch and sound,
no luminosity,
and Black paint
overtakes all other colors,
you can't find the others within,
and Blackness is like
multiplying anything with zero
you get zero,
blackness times anything
equals blackness.
Blackness births
black babies,
no matter the mate,
which is unfathomable to see
and see
Black people,
they were forced to live
non-transparently
if they wanted to survive,
which means other lives
had to have faith
that what was shared was
the honest truth that they
couldn't just outright see.
Engaging Blackness
requires some sense,

in fact, it requires
the other five senses,
faith being the greatest,
and Blackness
requires too much faith
that retribution
won't blindside
them when blinded,
so, Blackness instead
inspires fear.
Black people seem to scare
folks like black holes
and the blackest of nights do.
Black is deemed scary.
But black isn't scary,
its power is.
Black holes
are the epitome of gravity,
it attracts all to it,
that power is scary.
Black appears
even when the crayon is missing,
just mix enough
and it appears,
it manifests itself,
and that influential magic terrifies some.
Dominion lies
inside the black shadow
that cools when the sun
burns furiously,
some rather burn than
be soothed in something unknown.
And well,
Black people won't break
because they too are powerful.
Black holes

are beautiful.
Black crayons
are beautiful.
Black skies
are beautiful.
Black skin
is beautiful.
But black is
still tired.
Black holes are
tired of sucking up trash.
Black crayons are
tired of neglect.
Black nights are
tired of disapproval.
And Black lives are
tired of trying
to convince
anyone that they matter.
Black
is
tired.
But black
is always
resilient.
It is preeminent.
It can't and won't
disappear or dissipate.
It counters the darkness of light
with the lightness of the dark.
And no matter how tired
Black is,
it is
here to stay.

AN INTERROBANG WITH A SEMICOLON ENDING

Below the knee,
above the ankle
on the inner side of leg
it resides,
not so much for others' gaze,
though some
have paid tribute
with a sensual kiss, but
it's a reminder
for self,
to be seen
any time left is crossed over right
ankle on top knee.

It's an immediate call
to recall,
not of playing chicken
with dominating trains,
or the seduction from
the sensual sleepy siren,
pills, or the knife
that pleaded
"let me etch an eleven".

It's there
not for the almost conclusions,
the almost pauses in story,
but a memorial
for my lifelong friend
Ideation.

Ideation was a passive buddy
but my roll dawg
always

especially when none other was.
We passed letters with wishes of
being eternal roomies.
We grew
from children
to teens
to coworkers.
It was complicated.
Codependent likely.

Never a healthy relationship —
which of mine
has ever been?

Can't pour some out for it,
too busy ingesting each sip,
it's the only way to cope with the loss,
lest I sit in it.
Sitting in the darkness is...

I stare at it,
on my inner left leg,
above my ankle,
a sexy and secret spot.

I hear my late friend's voice
as I stare at its tribute.

...contemplating...

They say
resilience
comes when letting thoughts go,
when dismissing the unhealthy,
when attempting to forge forward,
maybe
that's why
mid a rollercoaster life
appeared the semicolon tattoo.

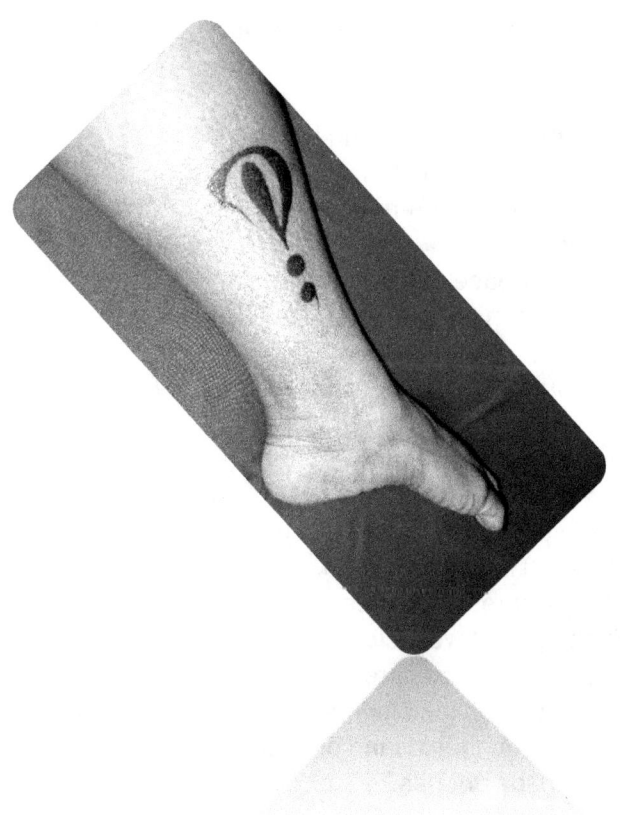

IN THE ZENDO 3-12-24

Back in the zendo;
it is normally a yoga studio.
There are still eight sconces,
two on each wall of the square.
There are four chandeliers
with five lights making twenty and
the windows are still playing make believe
in all their almost stained-glass glory.

Did not reclaim my seat
under the sixth webbed sconce.
It was taken when I arrived.
No death trap hovered seats for me...
I sit by the door.

While others meditate, I pray like Celie.
May God make bird of me.
This fly ass fly-in-the-milk shit is
exhausting.
I came for peace, ease, to escape
not for more nice violence.

If the point of the book discussed
was as big as Kincaid's small island,
they managed to miss it.
They were too busy
wearing their tourist-colored shades
on ravaged Indigenous land.
Only we oppressed notice.
Only those that work closely
with the oppressed care,
the others book their flights
to the next occupied land on their
Congo-made phones.

I whisper to the other person of color
who struggled to come to terms,
"this 'refuge' always has been
landmines and hanging death traps."

1970s DANGEROUS

Two friends of friends
were pushed in front of trains,
one a woman,
one a man,
both made the news.
Another friend of a friend
was murdered by "do gooders"
on the train, too.
He also made the news.

The word is,
trains are 1970s dangerous.
You gotta be prepared
like the woman
who defended her friend.
The attacker brought a gun
to the fist fight
turned knife fight
turned death match.
The aggressor was no match.

When asked,
"What is going on in the subways?"
The conductor said,
"What isn't?"
and shared the link to the vest,
soon to be placed between
undershirt and uniform,
between existence and demise
on the trains he so loved.

These rails raised us.

I, who used to ride at 1am

solo,
stop at 8.
I be ordinary,
but my temper be special.
It be especially short
starting fights fists can't finish.
I'd easily be finished.
Fuses are short everywhere.
We're all sparks seeking kindling, or
kindlings awaiting sparks.
I stay at bay,
head in book or phone,
with third eye always aware.

Yet waving away someone's
vaped exhalation
once put me at risk.
The teens made a scene,
the largest in their group,
seated next to me,
played with his knife,
flicking it like a fidget spinner.
I pretended not to see —
closely watching.

This was 4pm.
It was 9:40am for Michelle.
It was 6:48pm for Jason.
It was rush hour for Jordan.

It was 8:08 this morning
when two changed the energy
on the rushed train.
One stood, wearing a gaiter,
carrying phone and speaker in hand,
with two fingers pointing

at the crown of his seated buddy.
They rapped along to the beats,
throwing signs and
gesturing.

I wanted to
warn them of the dangers down the track,
I wanted to
tell them to turn that music off, it was too early for that shit,
I wanted to
enfold them in the love they've been starved of.
I wanted to...

When...

Something slipped stealthy from
the sweats of the seated.
Neither noticed.
Helpful me almost pointed.
But I, too, saw nothing,
I said nothing.
The gesticulations suggested stillness,

still I was.

I lingered at our shared destination,
made sure not to cross the cats' paths.
And the nothing I saw laid there.
Camouflaged with the salt and pepper floor
was a black blade, forgotten.

New York trains are
1970s dangerous.

ELEVATED PLAYBOOK

A perfect number of 5,
including a weary elder with her cane
and myself, sleep still in eyes,
lined up, patiently, waiting,
with respectful distance.

All were highly favored with
varying shades of
sun-hugging skin.
A combed-over man came, left,
choosing stairs —
the wait too long.
My knee groaned.

A woman, older, stoutier
and less blessed
joined the line.
Like a thief, she tiptoed.
Distance mattered not.

With every step,
I stepped.
She pivoted,
I did also.

And as the doors opened,
my exhausted elder exclaimed,
"I can't believe this!"
noting the play being made.

Agreement shared.

Remembering football season began,
inspired by the gridiron warriors,
I ignore my pain,
extended my arm,
positioned my frame,
blocking the way of one,
defending the other.
Making sure her feet
touched down first.

The other got on, eventually,
squeezed in the claustrophobic corner,
no space offered in the back,
backed against wall,
as was her rightful place.
Was also the last to exit

as I wished my sweet elder
good day.

FOR EMMETT, DICK, HAYWOOD, AND ALL ACCUSED

On a sweltering Wednesday,
a non-sun tanning, only
bottle-tanning woman
stood boldly on a crowded train
ignorant of others' autonomy.
After attempting to Columbus
a West Indian woman's space and
assaulting an African American lady
no less than six times
with her unapologetic stumbles
and oversized seat-stealing handbag,
she coughed.

Her rendition of the tale spun:
she covered it.

The masked gay Black man, wiped his left arm,
proclaiming her nasty, stated otherwise.
He will confidently say she coughed on his arm.
Vapors making contact.
The heaviness of disrespect
splashing down on his dermis.

She repeated,
"I covered my cough?"

What she did was half ball a fist,
placed it distant from orifice,
and while facing him
freely sprayed her germs.

She claimed innocence,
exited the train, and her victims
remained just that...

SAME SHIT DIFFERENT PIGEON

In high school a pigeon shitted on me.
Actually, in high school,
several pigeons shitted on me...
See, while in high school,
I had an early morning class
that made me pass
under a flock of pigeons
right on time for their
morning movements.
And they didn't give a crap
that I was simply a studious student
headed downtown to school.
They targeted me as if
practicing for varsity.
Pigeons 5 me 0.
I can still recall
the unforgettable impact
of their poop plopping upon me.
Shit, they even got me on my face.
Splat!
On my face.
Strangers stared strangely at my face
as I tried to wipe away the disrespect.

They disrespected me constantly.
Which makes sense,
it was probably payback
for all those times that as a kid
I ran up on their flocks
just to make them fly,
just to make them scared,
just to see them at ill ease.
I was that kid,
that kid that was unafraid of pigeons

and who didn't realize that pigeons
had no fears either.
They were unphased by little me
or teen me.
They, be unbothered by us.
And this is probably why
most of us hate pigeons.
They boldly take up the space
we keep thinking is ours to claim.
Their gain in space is our loss
and we hate that.

If you google pigeons
you'll find 15 ways
to get them out of your yard or
9 ways to poison them
and not other birds.

Pigeons, therefore, get no respect.
They are flying rats.
Deserve only our refuse.
Such miscreants.

But they've been given a bad rap.

Pigeons have been labeled as dumb
but they are smarter than most.
Thought to be a modern problem
but they've been the answer for centuries.
And are blamed for causing disease
but can identify them before a spread.

Pigeons are marked for extinction
but they were forcibly brought here,
domesticated, used as pawns in war,
on Wall Street, for mail,

in races, for entertainment,
they were good,
then were good for
nothing.
Nothing.
Not one single thing
were they good for except
to take blame.
And I can't help but wonder
why?
Was it their gray feathers?
Their shadowy hue?
Was it?
What is it?

If we stopped calling them pigeons
and used their other name,
rock
DOVES,
if we acknowledged
that they, too, are doves
would they be loved more?
Would they finally
be invited to the weddings?
Given a place at the table?
Be fed more than scraps?
Seen as pure?
As symbols of peace?
Would we finally notice
the promise embedded
in their beautiful coats?
If we changed,
if you changed,
would they finally matter?

WHY COME?

If a butterfly fluttered
and no one witnessed it
does it not have an effect?

If you get woozy post
consuming a Cosby Special
were you not drugged?

If someone changed the terms of consent
by removing the barrier or
poking holes,
was that not also a crime?

If a person describes an act as rape
without calling it rape,
were they not still raped?

Then how come,
when a wealthy man,
with a bodyguard outside the door,
coerced a woman into sex
we call it a "stormy" time in her life.

And why come when a man
stood between me and the exit
pursuing/pressuring until my no eroded,
all the time not noticing or caring
that I blank-faced disassociated
while he associated himself with my shell,
why come the male officer
called it buyer's remorse?
How was that not rape?
The consent was confiscated,
not enthusiastically established.

Was that not then rape?

If 1 in 5 women and
1 at 7 men report sexual assaults but
few accused see prisons' interiors,
does that make 57 million people in the US liars?

Then tell me how and why
some men don't understand
the reasons behind
women, men, trans or otherwise
choosing a field of beasts
than meeting a strange man
in the woods, parking lot,
alley, on the job, or
at the front door.

We'd rather be savagely ravaged
than live with the trauma of the encounter.

NOTHING IS

The great no-shots-held
Nikki Giovanni said,
we be hypertensive,
not because of our seasonings but
because of the tears never released.
I am happy to announce
I have a headache today
after crying all yesterday.
My pressure is more normal.
Emphasis on more.
Nothing is normal.
Nothing will ever be normal.

MY AWARD WINNER

The last five
American poet laureates
wrote about birds,
they have a bevy of work
about birds.
Apparently,
the only way to become a poet of note
is to cage birds on our pages.
I ask,
do poems
about the chicks 'round my way count?
They were fierce,
fiery and
fly.

Would a poem
about my godmother
calling us two kids chickadees do?
Or something written about that scene
in Back to the Future 2
when faxes flew at Marty McFly
after he did something against policy
in response to being called,
"chicken?"
Would that work?

Or

should I write a poem
about being today years old
when discovering
the origin of the phrase
chicken head?...
It makes so much more sense now.

I'm so bird-brained sometimes.

Would those bird poems count?

Or should I write about
the infirmed man,
living alone in a cluttered room
within a famous long stay hotel
with his many birds
that I delivered a meal to
on Thanksgiving?

Is that compelling?

What about a poem
about the weathered woman
that always brought her only friend,
a parrot,
to our Wednesday prayer groups
until it got sick?

Or a poem
about a pigeon
eating a piece of chicken
that caused me to question
if they were cannibals or
if they were just another cautionary tale
of what being at the bottom
of the capitalist ladder
will do to one's soul?
Feral pigeons are, after all,
byproducts of this society
just like my ancestors,
just like me.

Or does that other poem work,
you know,
the one I wrote about
the gaggle of geese
that flew in the wrong direction
to escape the cold
because that pandemic had us all so fucked up
that Baby Boomers and Gen Xers
lost their bearings...

Will that garner me an award?
Will this poem garner me an award
or like my skin,
are these birds not cared about either?

THE GRAVEYARD

If
watching trauma
triggers decades old
PTSD and shortens
lifespans
just for having
witnessed atrocities
on tiny screens
while hearing the
pops and
screams and
last gasps,

How
many grays
have I gained
mourning over
the graves
of the many
that look like me?
How many grays
were gained and
days lost when
repetitiously witnessing
people
as their souls
left bodies
that resembled mine?

Did
the black strands
turn gray
as life drained out
of black bodies

that too
became grayer?

Should
I name each
follicle changed
after those slain
at the hands of those
that
claimed authority
over a Black life
that required
their gray death,
those we
lost
when others
wielded power over
black and gray?

Is
the newest patch of gray
for Ahmaud, Breonna,
Marcus-David, Sonya, Jonathan,
Rayshard, W Wallace, Robert B,
and the over 160 others?

Shall
I place flowers
at my tombstone roots
in memoriam of all?

AND IF THIS WHOLE EXPERIENCE WASN'T A METAPHOR...

100 beats per minute...
that's my heart,
speeding,
always,
even when resting,
except during the 4 to 5 hours
of sleep I get where
I slow my mind enough
to stop my body from
reflexively running,
because clearly my heart is racing
like it were a rat trying to win or
is it the blood cells in my veins
that are attempting to run away
knowing they are being hunted.

Doctors for years have
dismissively said
my heart was rushing.
Rushed each time
they monitor it.
Maybe it was rushing
the appointment's end,
rushing out of their chair,
or off their table.
Possibly rushing with
the anxiety caused
by visiting a medical system
that seldom treated me properly.
No one ever tried to slow it or
investigated the cause,
it was just my normal,
as was my anemia.

Despite always being
challenged and sharpened
my iron was
markedly
diminished.

My white male primary doctor
was so worried that he eagerly,
excitedly and repeatedly
scoped and probed my intestines
to make sure there was
no internal bleeding.
There was no bleeding there
so he stopped caring
about my care.

My non-Black GYN tried to warn me
that fibroids might be
killing me slowly.
She advised me
eat dark greens
and red meat and
told of a patient
that was almost exsanguinated
as a cautionary tale...
but who has time for such tales
or sick time when bosses
request that you postpone surgery
and the price of curative meat
requires paychecks with more flexibility?

I heard the warning and kept on going,
kept on running myself ragged
because bootstraps cost money too
and I've been busy trying to pull

dreams into reality...
if I can just make it here,
I'll most certainly make it anywhere...

But my new Black doctor
connected the pieces
with one word.
Tachycardia.
She said my heart was racing
like the cops and the reaper were chasing
because my cup
was overflowing with blood
while my body
was failing to replenish its force,
my heart's been
working double its speed,
shortening my time...

No wonder I've been feeling
short on breath,
exhausted and
depleted and
like I'll never win...

And if this whole experience,
if my tachycardic heart,
wasn't an extended metaphor
I'm not sure what is.

RESPITE

My fatigued, urban-acclimated feet,
hurriedly stumbled through
the life restoring forest
rushing to where I could go for rest.
I desperately needed a respite.
And it was there, it was here,
among the trees that dwarfed me
that I paused,
though winded,
and stared into the atmosphere
hoping to escape that which I most fear,
the Olympic-sized weight of my race,
which is why I raced there
to erase the impact of my differences
just
for
a
moment.
I need
this
moment.
Don't ask me to return
and don't
placate me with your
soma flavored ice cream.
Can't you see that my eyes
scream and stream the hurt
that my words can't expel…

Is this a curse?

Are all that are born with black skin
trapped in a sin-fueled spell,
and we are the chosen victims?

This must be a curse?

Can you just let me sit here a spell,
please, and don't
tell me to sniff the lies-filled roses or
admire the deceitful tulips when
your two lips refuse
to acknowledge my existence.

Living as I do,
trying to peacefully exist
is just too fucking tense.

And that, that is why Deputy
Clyde Kerr, III
took his life.
Tightrope walking the razor's edge between
his black hue and his duty in blue,
he grabbed his life lines
from the hands of the Fates
sealing his own.
It was his form of empowerment,
after realizing that his
law enforcement power meant
he had none.

He, like me,
was tired of being a bounded pawn.
So...
he took control.
Videoed his swan song and then
like that
was gone.
He is gone.

But he couldn't see that he
was going to be the solution,
he was our greatest greatness,
his presence was beneficial,
but now we sing benedictions y'all...

And I just can't make this
make any kind of sense.

This world is so outstanding but
we Black folk get left standing out
on the picket lines alone, often
on the outs with the rest of society.

Treated always like we are cursed...

I don't want to be...
I just want to be...

...And after much thought
and consideration
and honestly
some contemplation
I now know that I don't want to escape like he or
take a Korryn Gaines' style last stand, but damn,
this truly is no easy plight,
and my body is weary from this fight
so I will still sometimes flee internally,
other times externally,
to the woods,
where my difference matters not,
and where I can dream up what
the what-coulds could be,

It's here that I grab pen
deep breathe the forest scene
and narrate new realities.

THE NIGHT THAT DIDN'T HAPPEN

A four-year-old didn't scream "Daddy?!"
And his fiancé didn't record
the aftermath of a tragedy.
And a series of pops didn't change worlds.
In fact, bullets didn't fly at all,
they rested in their magazine.
The day proved to be boring and
routine for a cop on his beat.

Philando, therefore, never
reached for his permit or license.
He was never stopped.
He never stopped.
He didn't stop.
He drove down the road
with his lady and their child
letting the latest music play as
backdrop to the requisite "talk".

Though summer, he dreamt of the fall
when all the children at the school
would smile as he served
warm meals that filled needy bellies.

And as a result of the quiet day,
I put the full bottle of pills down,
sleep feeling as if it will come easy
and assistance will not be needed,
momentary or permanent.

Rivers reverse their course,
then pool, then vanish
as if never there,
as if in defiance,
as if defying
the gravity of race relations.

And the late-night show
that could trigger
the contemplation to end it all
just joshes generally about fatherhood.
Nothing traumatizing or triggering
flashes across the screen

so I laugh, lightly at bad dad jokes,
and drift off safely
in my home and in my skin.

THIS VERY MOMENT
after "Be Real Black for Me" by Roberta Flack and Donny Hathaway

Today, do me a favor,
be you,
beautifully,
bewitchingly,
with no apologies,
no concerns,
no anything that doesn't serve you,
nothing unauthentic.

Today,
celebrate your ancestors
but not their traumas or grievances,
there's no space for that in this moment,
so leave the rules behind,
the straighten ups,
the masks,
the false tongues,
the forced smiles,
the anything that doesn't celebrate you.

Today,
walk in the sun and let it kiss you,
let it warm and nourish you,
love up on you,
it won't burn you,
it will honor you, hug you,
hug it back.

Today,
break every alarm clock,
move when you are ready,
don't even entertain CPTime jokes
instead,

move to the rhythm set by your internal drum,
listen to that,
feel it calling you,
let your appendages move with it,
when they so choose to.

Today,
smell your favorite scents,
let your nostrils rejoice with each inhalation,
let your lungs thank you
for the moments to savor such aromas.
Feast on your favorite seasonings,
let each taste bud delight at the invigorating flavors.
Remember, love your entire magnificent body,
spend time in the mirror.
Those parts named imperfections
are the souvenirs of your experiences,
thank them,
kiss them,
worship them,
dote upon them,
lay flowers at them in humble gratitude.

Today,
do me a favor,
celebrate the parts commonly told to hide,
find yourself lost in how enthralling you are,
silence the negative,
then pull up a chair and dine
in the kitchen at the back of your neck,
rest on the thickness of your lips,
ride the soothing waves of your hips,
gyrate all of you as your eyes roll,
be amused by the loudness of your voice,
strut your style in that color parade,
defy gravity with your sacred crown;

the everything you were told to hide
let it show out wild and with pride.

Do me this favor,
do yourself this favor,
do this,
even if you can't do it all days,
right now,
unapologetically,
be.
Celebrate.
Live here.
For this moment.
For as long as you need.
Breathe.
Be.
Be Black.
Be *real* Black,
And revel in whatever that means.

DREAMSCAPE

Normal,
they say normal is usual,
typical, expected,
it's the standard on which we stand,
it's what you know,
it's the constant condition.
It's the constant
in the condition.
They long for normal,
for the before,
the pre,
the days when the only thing masked
were intentions,
not faces,
though some of us
were masked every day,
the world demanded it and now
it demands for it again,
demands for days of
black and white where
white was idyllic and black…
black hung as tree ornaments,
or at least didn't protest for their life,
didn't interrupt the normal,
they just died like normal,
just like the kids in schools died
like normal,
because obsession with guns
was normal.
They want this normal back,
the one where forced sterilization
was so normal it didn't make the news
and where women lost their rights
to dictate their own life.

This, this is the standard
in which they rush back to,
where viruses
didn't make us pause and see
the inequality in our realities,
where pre-existing conditions were
created, generated
to be a norm that was unspoken of,
where normal, where status quo
collected casualties silently.
They say they want normal,
you know the normal where
our smog hid mountains
and muffled birds.
They want the absurd that they knew,
they want nothing new that feels insane.
That feels insane,
feels like they'd rather stick to a mundane
as a way to limit progress the same way they used to;
small bites
their bodies could digest,
small thoughts
their minds could process,
small steps
that moved so slowly
time reversed itself,
regressed
back to days that weren't sweet
for the global majority,
weren't great for those deemed
"minorities",
but this, this is the normal they seek,
an unmasked normalcy.
It seems abnormal to me,
and I want no part
in their normal fallacies.

NO SOLICITING

Don't come looking for me
on your picket lines or
at your protests.
I won't be there.
I won't be bolstering your numbers.
Keep your feminist movements,
as if you haven't already.
I won't be swooping in
to rescue your next failed march,
just to be ousted moments later.

Don't come crying to me
about your injustices,
about your oppressions,
and save your tears,
lest for my kettle,
for they are not my kryptonite.

Don't look for me when
your solid rock proves sinking sand,
after you slung your feces at the fan,
after you tried drowning me
when I last tried rescuing you.
You get no second chances.

And don't come to me for any pathy
except apathy,
symp or emp,
don't exist for you.
I ran out of them
when my fucks cup depleted.

And when one of my kind
does not cosign your ledger of nonsense,
look not to me either.
I am not going to be
the nice one, the good one,
the palatable one,
the one that makes sense.
I will shatter your ego,
shred your pride,
I will verbally eviscerate you.
Don't come here.

And don't send your kids either,
not for milk,
for their hair,
or their safety.
I'm not your hired hand,
nor am I your unpaid aide.
I retired my apron and cape.
Consider me
the antihero in your story.
You best start lactating,
attend Internet University,
and watch your own offspring.

I will no longer show you
how to bathe,
what not to ingest, or
even place on your face.
Natural selection shall have its way.
May the odds be
never
in your favor.
I am done assisting,
proceed as if I don't exist.

This is my last warning.

Do not look in this direction
for your next instructions.
Do not knock on my door.
Do not slide pamphlets
to my side of anything.
Do not even dare take a step
onto this property.
I am over you —
done expelling energy on the foolish.

I told you too many times,
damn near dragged you
by your greasy threads
to the precipice of the to come
and you said, "but my man..."
shuttering ears,
heeding to no cautioning,
you knew better.

Now that we are here,
uteruses monitored,
voting rights shriveling,
literal shit on faces,
do not ask me for anything.
I will be busy, surviving.

Do not come looking for me.

ACKNOWLEDGEMENTS

I give honor, praise, and gratitude to God for blessing me with the ability to turn my experiences and observations into stories that resonate. Writing has been my way of making sense of the world, of giving shape to emotions, of leaving something meaningful behind.

This book wouldn't exist without the love and encouragement of the people around me. To my mom, Darlene, and my father, Arthur—you have been my foundation. And to my brothers, Cairo, David, and Ray—you've cheered me on, pushed me forward, and believed in me even when I doubted myself. I'm endlessly grateful for each of you.

To Sapphyra, Ena, Kameron, Alejandro, and Sofia—you remind me daily why it's worth striving to make the world a little better. And to my mentees, TR and SD—I hope I've been able to offer you even a fraction of the inspiration you've given me.

A special thanks to my fellow writers and poets—those who've written with me, challenged me, inspired me, and given me space to perform. The late Bobby Gonzalez, Leah V, Kevin Powell, Mo Beasley, Natalie Goldberg, the Black Authors Collaborative, Poetix University, The HoneyDrippers Poetry Collective (especially The Anthology), Friday Night Writes, Creative Expressions, The College Club Crew, Sari-Sari, and Women Writers in Bloom Poetry Salon—you've shaped the artist I've become, and I carry pieces of you in my work.

To my incredible support system: Ajha F, Catherine M, Catherine S, Corinne S, Courtney N, Ginny S, Jenique J, Jereni-Sol, Jerry F, Jim M, Kesi G, Kimma B, Michael C, Michael M, Moses H, Nupur NB, Omar P, Paco I, Symone E, Talib H, Tammy L, and my Alaska, Church, and NUL families—your kindness, your belief, your presence mean everything. To my extended family, dear friends, and colleagues, you are woven into this journey. I may not name you all but trust me when I say the gratitude is limitless.

And finally, Tonii Langhorne—thank you for seeing me, for believing in me, for pushing me toward my potential. To DeAndre King, Douglas Cala, Krystal Kavita Jagoo, Pamela "Rare Epiphany" Best, and Ty Black—thank you for helping me reach the finish line when I needed that final push.

This book is more than words on a page—it's a reflection of everyone who has been part of my path. I hope it stirs something in you, inspires you, challenges you, or simply reminds you that you are seen.

AUTHOR'S OTHER WORKS

If you enjoyed this book and would like to further support this author or read more of Dara Kalima's literary works, you are invited to purchase any of her previous books listed below:

Black Man, Black Woman, Black Child
Casualty of Love
Two X Chromosomes with an Extra Shot of Melanin
Still Laughin'

Dara's work also appears in the following anthologies:

Women of Eve's Garden, Gathering of the Tribes, 2018
Bleed Anthology, ii Publishing, 2020
Moist Anthology, ii Publishing, 2020
2020: The Year That Changed America, kepo Inc., 2021
A Shape Produced by a Curve, Great weather for MEDIA, 2023
Which Side Are You On? Labor Day 2023, Moonstone Press, 2023
Freedom 2024, Moonstone Press, 2024
Happy 90th: A Tribute to Sonia Sanchez, Moonstone Press, 2024
Renascentem: Crow Calls Volume VI, Quill & Crow Publishing House, 2024
Sweat, BarBar, 2024
Whisper Whisper Shout, When Women Speak Publications, 2025

All books can be purchased at your local bookseller of choice. Please spread the word with your networks.

ABOUT THE AUTHOR

Dara's writing journey shifts depending on the context. At eight, she typed out her first short story in her Bronx home, perfecting it with her mother's help before sharing it with classmates. By sixteen, she embraced poetry and co-founded a local youth theater. At twenty-five, she set writing goals—mostly for poetry.

In high school, she penned satirical pieces for the yearbook. In college, while earning her BA in Literature with a Drama Studies concentration, she explored short story writing. But despite earning good grades, a disapproving remark led her to abandon prose and channel her creativity into poetry.

Her academic path led to an MA in Educational Theater and an MPA in Nonprofit Administration. Though her career focused on numbers, data, and events, poetry remained a quiet force until she publicly debuted her craft in 2015 with *Black Man, Black Woman, Black Child*. Since then, she has published three poetry collections, a memoir, and edited numerous works.

Now, with thousands of poems, blog entries, and personal reflections, Dara's artistry continues to challenge norms, spark healing, and foster critical conversations. This dedication earned her the titles *The Community Poet* and *The Poetic Sadist*. She welcomes meaningful discussions—just know you might inspire her next creation.

www.ingramcontent.com/pod-product-compliance
Lightning Source LLC
LaVergne TN
LVHW051508070426
835507LV00022B/2989